FAR-OUT GUIDE
to the
SOLAR SYSTEM

FAR-OUT GUIDE TO

SATURN

Mary Kay Carson

Bailey Books
an imprint of
Enslow Publishers, Inc.
40 Industrial Road
Box 398
Berkeley Heights, NJ 07922
USA
http://www.enslow.com

For Rose Elizabeth Schelly, a jewel as sparkling as Saturn.

Bailey Books, an imprint of Enslow Publishers, Inc.

Copyright © 2011 by Mary Kay Carson

Library of Congress Cataloging-in-Publication Data
    Carson, Mary Kay.
    Far-out guide to Saturn / Mary Kay Carson.
        p. cm. — (Far-out guide to the solar system)
    Includes bibliographical references and index.
    Summary: "Presents information about Saturn, including fast facts, history, and technology used to study
the planet"—Provided by publisher.
    ISBN 978-0-7660-3178-4 (Library Ed.)
    ISBN 978-1-59845-187-0 (Paperback Ed.)
    1. Saturn (Planet)—Juvenile literature. 2. Solar system—Juvenile literature. I. Title.
    QB671.C367 2011
    523.46—dc22

                           2008050038

Printed in China

052010 Leo Paper Group, Heshan City, Guangdong, China

10 9 8 7 6 5 4 3 2 1

Image Credits: ESA – D. Ducros, p. 37; ESA/NASA/JPL/University of Arizona, pp. 38, 39; Karl Kofoed, p. 26;
NASA/CXC/M. Weiss, p. 12; NASA/David Seal, pp. 28–29; NASA, ESA and Erich Karkoschka (University of
Arizona), p. 6; NASA/JPL, pp. 1, 4–5, 8–9, 15, 16, 25, 34, 36, 40–41, 43; NASA/JPL/Space Science Institute, pp. 3,
7, 13, 17, 20, 31; NASA/JPL/University of Arizona, pp. 18, 35.

Cover Image: NASA/JPL

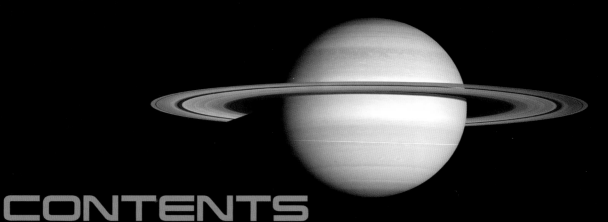

CONTENTS

INTRODUCTION
5

CHAPTER 1
THE RINGMASTER
8

SATURN AT A GLANCE
20

FAST FACTS ABOUT SATURN
21

SATURN TIMELINE OF
EXPLORATION AND DISCOVERY
24

CHAPTER 2
WORLDS OF WATER AND HAZE
27

CHAPTER 3
WHAT'S NEXT FOR SATURN?
40

WORDS TO KNOW
44

FIND OUT MORE
AND GET UPDATES
46

INDEX
48

SATURN is the sixth planet
from the Sun. (Note that the
planets' distances are not shown
to scale.)

Saturn

INTRODUCTION

No one is sure yet how many moons Saturn has. How is that possible? Scientists keep finding more! So far, astronomers have identified sixty-one moons circling Saturn. Better telescopes and recent spacecraft missions are helping them discover more moons. You will learn lots more far-out facts about Saturn in this book. Just keep reading!

Saturn is a stunning sight. The sixth planet easily earns its nickname: the jewel of the solar system. Its amazing rings are what make it so special. Saturn's rings shine and shimmer. They glow with stripes of colors highlighted with lines of shadow. The rings of Saturn make it the most recognizable planet after ours.

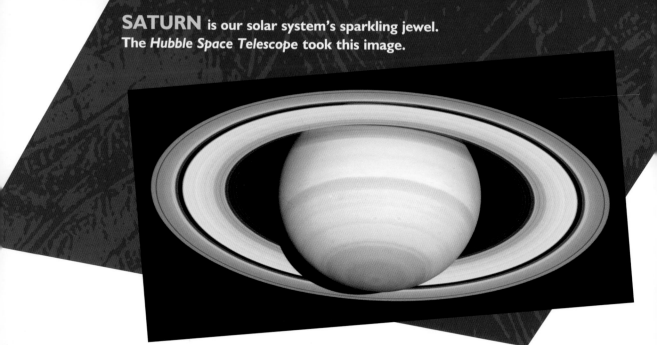

Everyone knows Saturn because of its rings. But those same rings hold many secrets. No one knows for sure when they started circling Saturn—or how they got there.

PRETTY MYSTERIOUS

Saturn is a planetary ball of liquids and gases called a gas giant. You could not stand on Saturn because there is no land or solid surface. It is a cold world with hurricane-like storms and fierce winds. At least sixty-one mysterious moons also circle Saturn. Many are small icy balls far from the planet, while others are squeezed between rings. Some of Saturn's moons even have water and other ingredients that life needs.

Scientists are working on solving Saturn's mysteries. A spacecraft that has recently been visiting Saturn has been a big help. *Cassini* has no crew. It is a robotic spacecraft, or space probe. *Cassini* began studying Saturn, its rings, and its moons in 2004. It has made many surprising discoveries about Saturn.

CASSINI took this picture when the Sun was behind Saturn. This view lights up Saturn's amazing rings from behind.

FAR-OUT FACT

HANDLES ON SATURN

When Galileo first observed Saturn in 1610, it confused him. The Italian astronomer could not clearly see the rings through his small telescope. He thought they looked like two large moons—one on each side of Saturn. A few years later, Galileo sketched Saturn's rings as loop-like teacup handles on either side of Saturn. In 1656, Christiaan Huygens got a better look using a more powerful telescope. The Dutch astronomer described what he saw as a thin, flat ring around the planet.

CHAPTER 1

THE RINGMASTER

Saturn is more than a planet. The enormous gas giant, its seven rings, and its sixty-one or more moons make up the Saturn system. Studying the Saturn system calls for a major mission and a large spacecraft. *Cassini* is both. It is the biggest space probe ever sent past Mars. *Cassini* left Earth in 1997. It took the robotic explorer seven years to reach Saturn.

SQUEEZING THROUGH

Cassini was not Saturn's first visitor. Three space probes flew by the ringed planet between 1979 and 1981. But *Cassini* was the first to study the sixth planet for a long time. *Cassini* is an orbiter, a space probe that circles around

THIS illustration shows the *Cassini* spacecraft arriving at Saturn. *Cassini* weighs 5,712 kilograms (12,593 pounds) and is about the size of a school bus.

a planet. When *Cassini* finally reached Saturn in 2004, it settled in for a long visit.

"Putting an orbiter around a planet and being able to hang out there" lets scientists watch Saturn, its moons, and its rings over time, says *Cassini* program scientist Carolyn Porco. Getting into orbit around Saturn was not easy, however. *Cassini* had to pass through the planet's rings first!

Saturn's seven rings are not solid. They are made up of billions of pieces of ice. The rings are like a hailstorm circling the planet in a wide, thin band. The rings stretch for a distance as wide as twenty-one Earths placed side by side. They're as thin as tissue paper compared to their width. Saturn's rings are only about twenty meters (sixty-five feet) or so thick. Some of the ice chunks that make up the rings are as big as a house. Others are as small as a single powdery snow crystal. "And they are screaming around the planet at 32,000 to 64,000 kilometers (20,000 to 40,000 miles) per hour," says Porco. It is a dangerous place for a spacecraft.

The plan was for *Cassini* to fly through a gap between two of Saturn's outer rings. Engineers hoped it could

FAR-OUT FACT

CASSINI

Cassini is named for the Italian astronomer Giovanni Domenico Cassini (1625–1712). He studied the Saturn system. Cassini discovered four moons and the gap between two major rings that is now named the Cassini Division. Scientists and engineers from seventeen different countries built *Cassini*. In 1997, a rocket launched the space probe. *Cassini* then began a 3.2-billion-kilometer (2-billion-mile), seven-year journey to Saturn. *Cassini* orbited Saturn for more than six years, making many important discoveries about the Saturn system.

safely pass through there. *Cassini* had to turn its antennae away from Earth before entering the rings. For ninety long minutes, the *Cassini* team was out of contact with the spacecraft. Then *Cassini* phoned home! *Cassini* had made it through the gap and slipped into orbit unharmed. (The illustration on page 15 shows where *Cassini* crossed between the rings.)

RINGING TRUTHS

No one was happier about *Cassini*'s success than Carolyn Porco. By the time the spacecraft reached the sixth planet, the astronomer had already spent fourteen years working on the mission. Porco's fascination with

THIS illustration shows the icy chunks that make up Saturn's rings.

Saturn goes back even farther. She caught her first glimpse of the ringed planet through a friend's telescope at age thirteen. It sparked a lifetime passion for astronomy. "To know that we can know so much about our solar system and about our cosmos, for me, makes life meaningful," says Porco.

Studying Saturn's rings is a big part of *Cassini*'s mission. "The questions that we scientists have about Saturn's rings are the questions that an ordinary person might . . . ask when first seeing them. . . . What

RINGS AROUND PLANETS

Saturn is known as the ringed planet, but it is not the only planet with rings. All four of the solar system's gas giant planets—Jupiter, Saturn, Uranus, and Neptune—have rings. Saturn's rings are so massive that they have been showing up in telescopes for centuries. The rings of the other planets couldn't be seen without better technology. Uranus's thin, icy rings were first seen in 1977 by astronomers using a telescope aboard an airplane. *Voyager I* discovered Jupiter's faint rings of rock and dust in 1979. And Neptune's dim rings were discovered in 1985.

caused them? How did they get there? How long have they been around? How long are they going to last?" says Porco. *Cassini* discovered that Saturn's rings are much younger than the planet. They likely came from a moon breaking up, or a comet crash. *Cassini* also found that the rings might be eroding away. As the rings' icy bits keep hitting each other and breaking up, they get smaller and smaller. The tiniest pieces are eventually lost into space.

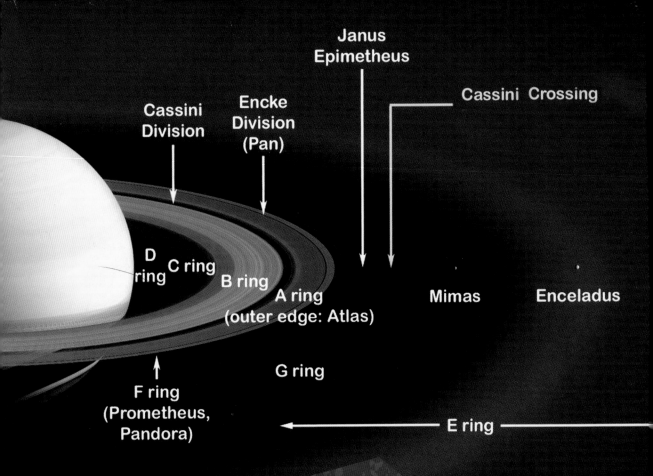

Janus
Epimetheus

Cassini Crossing

Cassini
Division

Encke
Division
(Pan)

D
ring

C ring

B ring

A ring
(outer edge: Atlas)

Mimas

Enceladus

G ring

F ring
(Prometheus,
Pandora)

E ring

SATURN'S SEVEN RINGS

Seven major rings make up Saturn's ring system. The rings
were named **A** to **G** in the order they were discovered. Starting
with the ring closest to Saturn, their order is **D, C, B, A, F, G,**
and **E**. The brightest rings are **B** and **A** and are separated by
a dark, 4,700-kilometer (2,920-mile) gap called the Cassini
Division. The **C** and **D** rings are closer to Saturn, but fainter.
The **F** ring is a narrow ring just outside the **A** ring. The **G** and
E rings are thicker, but very faint.

THIS *Cassini* image is color-coded to show how many particles of different sizes make up the rings. The white areas have the most particles. Purple areas have particles bigger than five centimeters (about two inches). Green areas have particles smaller than one centimeter (half an inch).

When will the rings completely disappear? "Hundreds of millions of years probably, maybe billions of years," says Porco. Scientists are still studying "whether the rings are young and are going to die an early death or they're old and going to remain with us a very very long time."

STORMY WEATHER

Cassini's mission includes watching weather on Saturn. Winds there can whip around at 1,600 kilometers (1,000 miles) per hour. That is three times faster than the strongest tornado winds! Clouds of snowy ice crystals float high in the atmosphere. Temperatures there dip down to more than one hundred below zero degrees Celsius (two hundred below zero degrees Fahrenheit). *Cassini* has found Saturn to be stormier than expected.

A powerful, long-lasting lightning-making storm in Saturn's storm alley rages in these two *Cassini* images. The left image is in true color. The right image is highlighted to make the storm easier to see.

Scientists even named one area of the planet "storm alley." There, oval-shaped storms "zip around . . . we watch them be created, we watch them die," says Porco.

One storm over Saturn's north pole has lasted a long time. The Voyager space probes first saw the oddly

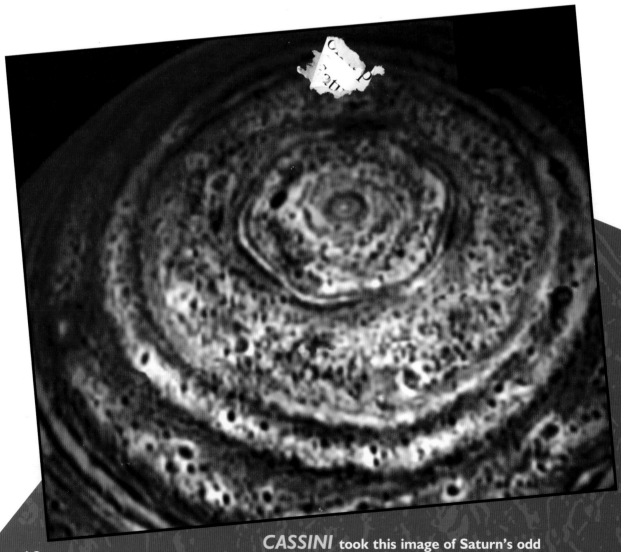

CASSINI took this image of Saturn's odd hexagonal storm in infrared light.

shaped storm in 1980 and 1981. *Cassini* found the same six-sided storm still there. The storm is the size of four Earths and has six straight sides, like a honeycomb hexagon. Scientists have never seen anything like it in the solar system. *Cassini* spotted another one-of-a-kind storm over Saturn's south pole. It is the only truly hurricane-like storm found on a planet other than Earth. Like Earth hurricanes, the Saturn storm has a hole, or an eye, surrounded by fast-spinning clouds. "Everyone got very excited about that," remembers Porco. "It even surprised us."

SATURN AT A GLANCE

Diameter: 120,536 kilometers (74,898 miles)

Volume: 764 Earths

Mass: 95 Earths, or 568,510,000,000,000 trillion kilograms

Position: Sixth planet from the Sun

Average Distance From Sun: 1,426,725,400 kilometers (885,904,700 miles)

Day Length: 10 hours, 39 minutes

Year Length: 10,756 Earth days (or about 29½ Earth years)

Color: Yellow with faint stripes

Atmosphere: 97 percent hydrogen; 3 percent helium

Surface: None

Temperature: -178 degrees Celsius (-288 degrees Fahrenheit)

Moons: At least 61

Rings: 7

Namesake: Roman god of agriculture

Symbol: ♄

Planet Fast Facts

★ Saturn is the second-largest planet in the solar system; only Jupiter is bigger.

★ The entire planet and all its rings would just fit between Earth and our moon.

★ Saturn is the least dense of all the planets and the only planet less dense than water. That means it would float in a gigantic tub of water.

★ It is the farthest planet you can see without a telescope and was the most distant planet until Uranus was discovered in 1781.

★ Like other gas giant planets, Saturn has no land or solid surface.

★ Saturn is a swirling ball of gas and high-pressure liquid.

★ Saturn is about 75 percent hydrogen and 25 percent helium, with tiny amounts of water, methane, and ammonia.

★ Winds around Saturn's equator reach speeds of 1,800 kilometers (1,118 miles) per hour. That is more than three times faster than the strongest tornado on Earth.

★ Thin clouds of water and ammonia create Saturn's bands of color.

★ The word *Saturday* comes from Saturn's Day, the name given to it by ancient Romans who believed Saturn controlled the day's first hour.

★ Saturn was named for the Roman god of agriculture.

Ring Fast Facts

★ Saturn's ring system is mostly made up of billions of icy bits with some dust and rock, too.

★ The rings wrap around Saturn's equator but do not reach the planet.

★ Countless tiny ringlets make up the seven main rings around Saturn.

★ The seven main rings have letter names. Ring A was the first discovered and G the most recently discovered.

★ Saturn's rings are each different. Ring F is narrow and ring B is wide, while ring D is faint and ring A is bright.

★ A new thick, see-though ring discovered in 2009 by the *Spitzer Space Telescope* is likely Saturn's largest ring of all.

★ Some ring particles are as small as snow crystals, while others are as big as a house.

★ Ring particles hurtle around the planet at speeds reaching 64,000 kilometers (40,000 miles) per hour.

★ Saturn has the most complex system of rings in the solar system. The rings extend many thousands of miles away from the planet and are less than one kilometer (half a mile) thick.

Moons Fast Facts

★ Astronomers have identified at least sixty-one moons around Saturn, but more small moons will likely be discovered someday.

★ Saturn's ten largest moons are Titan, Rhea, Iapetus, Dione, Tethys, Enceladus, Mimas, Hyperion, Phoebe, and Janus.

- ★ Titan is the second-largest moon in the solar system, after Jupiter's Ganymede.

- ★ Titan has an atmosphere similar to early Earth's.

- ★ Enceladus has gas-spewing geysers on its surface.

- ★ Pan is the closest moon to Saturn. It orbits within Saturn's main rings.

- ★ Phoebe orbits Saturn in the opposite direction of the planet's other large moons.

- ★ Mimas has a giant crater on one side, likely from an impact.

- ★ Sixteen of Saturn's moons keep the same side toward the planet as they orbit, just like Earth's moon.

Mission Fast Facts

- ★ In 1979, *Pioneer 11* was the first spacecraft ever to visit Saturn.

- ★ The *Voyager 1* and *Voyager 2* flyby space probes discovered that Saturn's rings were mostly ice.

- ★ The *Cassini* spacecraft successfully flew through the gap between two of Saturn's outer rings.

- ★ *Cassini* traveled at 114,000 kilometers (70,700 miles) per hour during its seven-year journey to Saturn.

- ★ *Cassini* flew by Venus and Jupiter on its way to Saturn.

- ★ *Huygens* was the first spacecraft to land on an outer solar system world when it touched down on Titan in 2005.

Saturn Timeline
of Exploration and Discovery

1610—Galileo sees Saturn's rings but is not sure what they are.

1650s—Christiaan Huygens identifies a thin, flat ring around Saturn and discovers Saturn's moon Titan.

1671–1672—Giovanni Cassini discovers moons Iapetus and Rhea.

1675—Giovanni Cassini discovers a gap between two of Saturn's rings, later named the Cassini Division.

1684—Giovanni Cassini discovers moons Dione and Tethys.

1789—William Herschel discovers moons Mimas and Enceladus.

1848—William and George Bond and William Lassell discover moon Hyperion.

1856—James Clerk Maxwell demonstrates that Saturn's rings are made of many circling objects, not one solid ring.

1898—William Pickering discovers moon Phoebe.

1966—Moons Janus and Epimetheus are discovered.

1979—Flyby probe *Pioneer 11* is first to visit Saturn, passing within 21,000 kilometers (13,000 miles) of its cloud tops; studying its atmosphere, temperature, and magnetic field; taking pictures of the planet and some of its moons; and discovering the thin F ring.

1980—Flyby probe *Voyager 1* passes within 64,200 kilometers (40,000 miles) of the planet's cloud tops, takes 16,000 images, and flies by Titan and other moons.

1981—Flyby probe *Voyager 2* flies within 41,000 kilometers (25,400 miles) of Saturn's cloud tops and studies the structure of the ring system, the planet's atmosphere, and the magnetic field. The Voyager probe images help scientists discover eight new moons and many smaller ringlets within Saturn's rings.

1990—*Hubble Space Telescope* observes a giant storm.

1994—*Hubble Space Telescope* makes images of some of Titan's surface.

2004—Orbiter *Cassini* begins orbiting Saturn, studying the entire Saturn system—planet, rings, and many moons. It makes lots of discoveries, including six new moons, salty water geysers on Enceladus, methane lakes on Titan, rings around Rhea, hurricane-like and hexagonal storms on Saturn, and many more.

2005—Probe *Huygens* (released from *Cassini*) studies Titan's atmosphere and sends back pictures from the giant moon's surface.

2005—Astronomers discover twelve new moons using ground-based telescopes.

2009—*Spitzer Space Telescope* discovers a nearly invisible gigantic ring around Saturn.

2020—Mission to orbit Titan and flyby Enceladus are set to launch.

GEYSERS on the surface of Saturn's moon Enceladus shoot out jets of water in this illustration.

CHAPTER 2

WORLDS OF WATER AND HAZE

Saturn's many moons come in all sizes. Titan is the extra large moon. It is bigger than Mercury. Many of Saturn's moons are small chunks of rocky ice the size of towns. Some medium-sized moons circle Saturn, too. Moons like Rhea, Iapetus, Dione, Tethys, Enceladus, Mimas, Hyperion, and Phoebe are not tiny, but they are smaller than Earth's moon. Enceladus is a medium-sized moon that scientists are giving an extra large amount of attention. It is bursting with surprises.

HOW MANY MOONS DOES SATURN HAVE?

Saturn's ten largest moons were mostly discovered long ago. (See the "Saturn Timeline of Exploration and Discovery" on page 24.) When the Voyager space probes arrived in the 1980s, they discovered eight new moons. This meant Saturn's moon total was eighteen when *Cassini* launched in 1997. Ten years later there were sixty-one known moons of Saturn. Giant telescopes on Earth discovered thirty-seven of the new moons. *Cassini* found another six moons during its mission. There are likely more small moons waiting to be discovered.

Mimas   Enceladus   Tethys   Dione   Rhea

MOON GEYSERS

In 2005, the *Cassini* spacecraft flew by Enceladus. It is an ice-covered world the size of Arizona. Scientists were shocked to see geysers shooting up from Enceladus's surface. "That was just mind blowing," says Cassini scientist Carolyn Porco. *Cassini's* instruments reported that the geysers are jets of ice crystals and water vapor.

THIS illustration compares the sizes of Saturn's nine largest moons. They are shown in their order from Saturn, left to right, though other, smaller moons come between them.

Hyperion

Phoebe

Titan

Iapetus

They erupt from pockets of salty liquid water not too far beneath the surface. The geyser jets shoot out of giant cracks around the moon's south pole.

How can water be liquid on a frigid –201 degrees Celsius (–330 degrees Fahrenheit) moon? Scientists are not exactly sure yet. Their best guess is a kind of friction. Saturn's gravity constantly pulls and tugs at Enceladus. So does the gravity of neighbor moon Dione. All this pulling and tugging shifts and moves Enceladus's ice, creating friction. Like rubbing your hands together, friction heats things up. If Enceladus's insides are shifting and rubbing together, the friction could be melting ice into pockets of underground ocean.

Cassini went back for a closer look in 2008. It swooped in, flying fifty kilometers (thirty miles) above Enceladus's surface. *Cassini* flew right through the geyser jets. The spacecraft found more than water in the foggy jets. Simple organic chemicals—the kinds all living things are built out of—were shooting off the moon, too. Enceladus could have the ingredients needed to support life: heat, water, and organic chemicals. Our ultimate goal is "[t]o go and seek out those environments in the solar system

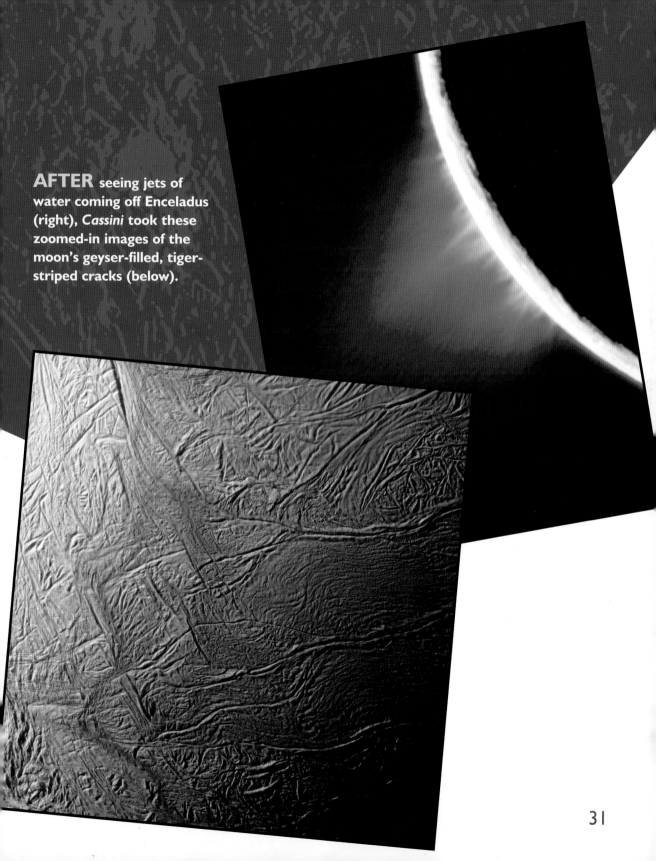

AFTER seeing jets of water coming off Enceladus (right), *Cassini* took these zoomed-in images of the moon's geyser-filled, tiger-striped cracks (below).

where life might possibly have gotten started and we just stumbled upon it," says Porco. "It's just one of those discoveries that you're not going to make often in your lifetime."

PROBING A GIANT

Titan is a place scientists have long wondered about. Christiaan Huygens discovered the giant moon more than 350 years ago. *Voyager 1* only made scientists more curious about Saturn's largest moon. (See "*Voyager* to Titan" on page 34.) When planning *Cassini's* mission,

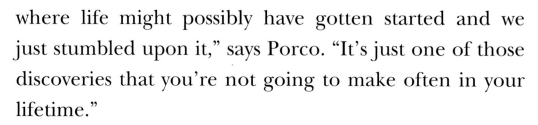

FAR-OUT FACT

RINGS AROUND RHEA

Cassini added another amazing find among Saturn's middle-sized moons. Rhea is likely circled by rings of its own. A disk of pebble- to boulder-sized rubble surrounds Rhea. There is a dust cloud beyond that. Instruments on board *Cassini* spotted as least one ring within the rubble and dust. Rhea is 1,500 kilometers (950 miles) wide and covered in craters. It is the first moon ever found to have rings.

OTHER ODD WORLDS

Saturn's sixty-one or more moons and seven rings make it a busy place. Moons Janus and Epimetheus occasionally pass so close to each other that they switch orbits. The moon Pan orbits within the A ring. Its gravity sweeps away ring particles, creating a clear path in the ring called the Encke Gap. Mimas, Enceladus, Tethys, Dione, and Rhea orbit within the faint, cloudy E ring. Prometheus and Pandora are called shepherd moons. They orbit inside and outside the F ring. Their gravity herds the ring's particles together.

Titan topped everyone's list of places to visit. Engineers gave the spacecraft haze-cutting radar to see Titan's surface. And they built *Huygens,* a separate probe to land on Titan. *Huygens* hitched a seven-year ride to the Saturn system. Then, in December 2004, the *Huygens* probe separated from *Cassini* and headed toward Titan.

John Zarnecki led the *Huygens* design team. Seeing Yuri Gagarin—the first human in space—inspired Zarnecki to study science. "As an 11-year-old schoolboy, I stood a few feet away from him when he visited London in 1961, as

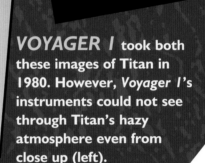

VOYAGER 1 took both these images of Titan in 1980. However, *Voyager 1*'s instruments could not see through Titan's hazy atmosphere even from close up (left).

VOYAGER TO TITAN

The robotic space probe *Voyager 1* was the first to fly by Titan in 1980. It found a haze-covered, cold world. Titan is the only known moon with a thick nitrogen atmosphere. Earth's atmosphere is 78 percent nitrogen, and Titan's is 95 percent nitrogen. Titan may be similar to Earth's early atmosphere before plant life added oxygen to our air. The spacecraft flew within 4,000 kilometers (2,485 miles) of Titan's surface. Unfortunately, *Voyager 1*'s cameras could not see through Titan's haze to the moon's surface.

the most famous man in the world," remembers Zarnecki. "His space achievement dazzled me." By the time *Huygens* separated from *Cassini,* Zarnecki had spent sixteen years working on the project. The final months of waiting were a tense time. "Titan . . . is very, very far away," Zarnecki told reporters in 2004. "This is going to be our only shot at it for an extremely long time."

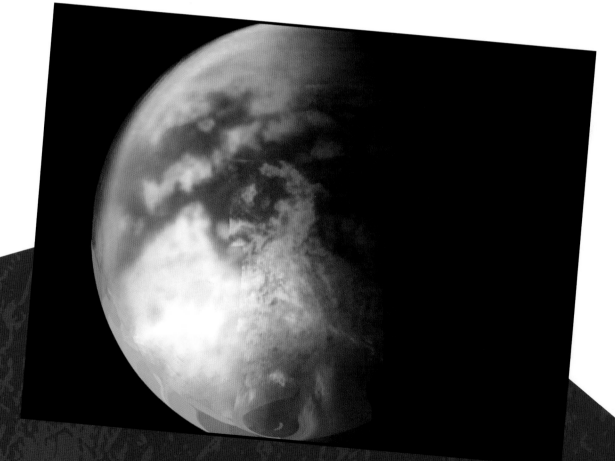

CASSINI'S radar cut through Titan's hazy atmosphere. Underneath is a surface of lakes, hills, dunes, and riverbeds.

DISTANT MOON LANDING

On January 14, 2005, *Huygens* plowed into Titan's atmosphere at six times the speed of sound. It popped its parachute and began taking weather measurements. As the probe floated down through the thick air, *Huygens* started snapping photos. The views were astonishing. The images showed a world covered in rocky hills with gullies. Titan has long chains of dunes, valleys, and canyons. As *Huygens* neared the surface, a shoreline appeared in the distance. The surface got closer and closer until *Huygens* set down with a gentle thud. *Huygens* had landed safely on Titan!

ENGINEERS attach the gold, saucer-shaped *Huygens* probe to *Cassini* in 1997.

THIS illustration shows the stages as *Huygens* parachutes through Titan's atmosphere and lands.

HUYGENS TO TITAN

The *Huygens* probe was named after Titan's discoverer, Dutch astronomer and mathematician Christiaan Huygens. The saucer-shaped spacecraft attached to the side of *Cassini*. The European Space Agency (ESA) built *Huygens*. Six instruments were on board to study Titan's atmosphere and surface. *Huygens* parachuted through the atmosphere recording sounds, taking images, and measuring winds and weather. Engineers mainly built *Huygens* as an atmospheric probe. But it lasted for ninety minutes on Titan's high-pressure surface.

The scene from the landed probe looked strange to scientists, yet familiar. The probe had landed in a flat area littered with rocks. Low hills lined the horizon. The sky above was an orange haze. Instruments aboard *Huygens* reported the surface was an icy, pudding-like, wet mud. "We're sitting on icy grains, which have the consistency of sand," Zarnecki told reporters. *Huygens* had landed in a dry riverbed. Just beneath the surface was a pool of liquid methane. Methane is natural gas—the gas used in cooking stoves. Titan is so cold that its methane is chilled to liquid. Liquid methane rains down and fills the lakes on Titan. No water falls from the orange sky. On Titan's surface, cold temperatures freeze water into

THIS is the Titan landscape *Huygens* saw as it fell toward the surface.

THIS is the scene *Huygens* saw at its landing site on Titan. The probe set down in a dry riverbed scattered with rocks made of water ice and hills in the distance.

rock-hard ice. It is flowing liquid methane that carves the riverbeds, lakes, and rain-washed gullies on Titan.

Huygens's mission on Titan was spectacular, but short. As expected, the probe only survived one-and-a-half hours under Titan's crushingly heavy air. But *Cassini* kept flying by the giant moon. In 2008, the Saturn orbiter found evidence of an underground ocean below Titan's icy surface. This ocean may be liquid water, warmed by Titan's hot center. If this is true, underground Titan will have those special ingredients for life—heat, liquid water, and organic chemicals (methane). Only a closer look will say for sure. "We've got to go back again with balloons and rovers and really understand this place," said Zarnecki.

CHAPTER 3

WHAT'S NEXT FOR SATURN?

Studying the information, pictures, and measurements from *Cassini* and *Huygens* will keep astronomers busy for years. Scientists will keep studying the space probes' findings for more clues about the sixth planet, its rings, and its mysterious moons. "It's quite complex," *Cassini* scientist Carolyn Porco says. "It'll take us a long time to figure it all out, and I don't think we'll ever figure *all* of it out." Meanwhile, more spacecraft missions to the Saturn system are being planned.

THIS illustration shows what
a possible future orbiting space
probe at Titan might look like.

LIFE IN THE DARK

A big part of scientists' interest in Titan and Enceladus is the chance that life exists there. *Cassini* found evidence that both moons have what it takes for life to start—heat, organic chemicals, and liquid water. How can worlds with so little sunshine have life? Not all ecosystems depend on green plants. Even on Earth some life exists without sunshine. Deep in Earth's oceans, there are microbes that exist on the chemicals from undersea volcanoes. These microbes are in turn food for tubeworms, clams, shrimp, and other creatures that never see sunshine.

ORBITING TITAN

The amazing discoveries on Titan and Enceladus make them major targets for another mission. The next spacecraft to study Titan will likely be one that sticks around—an orbiter. The Titan Saturn System Mission (TSSM) has just such a plan. If chosen for launch, it would likely leave Earth around 2020. The mission would have two parts. The main spacecraft would be an orbiter.

It would likely first orbit Saturn, making close-up flybys of Enceladus. Then it would go into orbit of Titan.

Attached to the main orbiter spacecraft would be a Titan probe—much like *Huygens* was on *Cassini*. Once near the giant moon, the Titan probe would separate from the orbiter and go down to Titan. What kind of probe would explore Titan's surface is not decided yet. Current plans being studied involve a lander and a balloon. The balloon could circle Titan beneath its haze and take weather measurements. The lander would hopefully study a methane lake and Titan's soil. What do you think it might find?

THIS illustration shows a balloon explorer floating over a lake of liquid methane on Titan. The winds on Titan would push a balloon completely around the globe in about six months.

Words to Know

astronomy—The study of moons, planets, stars, galaxies, and the universe.

atmosphere—The gases that surround a planet, a moon, a star, or another object in space that are kept around it by the object's gravity.

atmospheric probe—A space probe that studies the atmosphere of a planet or moon while passing through it.

comet—A large chunk of frozen gases, ice, and dust that orbits the Sun.

craters—Bowl-shaped holes made by explosions on the surface of a planet or moon, often from comet or asteroid crashes.

diameter—A straight line through the center of a sphere.

engineer—Someone who designs machines.

flyby probe—A space probe that flies by a planet or moon.

gas giant—A planet made of mostly gas and liquid with no land, such as Jupiter, Saturn, Uranus, and Neptune.

gravity—The force of attraction between two or more bodies due to their mass.

lander—A space probe that sets down on the surface of a planet or other object in space.

magnetic field—The area of magnetic influence around a magnet, an electric current, or a planet.

mass—The amount of matter in something.

methane—Natural gas, or a gas made of a combination of carbon and hydrogen.

microbe—A living thing too small to be seen without a microscope.

orbit—The looping path followed by a planet, a moon, or another object in space.

orbiter—A space probe that orbits a planet, a moon, or another object in space.

organic chemicals—Chemicals that have carbon atoms and can occur in living things.

planet—A large, sphere-shaped object in space that is alone (except for its moons) in its orbit around a sun.

pressure (atmospheric)—The force on a surface from the weight of the air above it.

ring—A thin band of dust, rocks, and ice particles orbiting around a planet.

shepherd moon—A moon that orbits near a ring's edge and whose gravity keeps ring particles from escaping.

solar system—The Sun and everything that orbits it.

space probe—A robotic spacecraft launched into space to collect information.

space telescope—A telescope that orbits Earth or travels in space.

volume—The amount of space something fills.

year—The time it takes for an object in space to travel around the Sun.

Find Out More and Get Updates

BOOKS

Aguilar, David A. *11 Planets*. Washington, D.C.: National Geographic, 2008.

Bortolotti, Dan. *Exploring Saturn*. New York: Firefly, 2003.

Carson, Mary Kay. *Exploring the Solar System: A History With 22 Activities*. Chicago: Chicago Review Press, 2008.

Croswell, Ken. *Ten Worlds*. Honesdale, Pa.: Boyds Mills Press, 2007.

Miller, Ron. *Saturn*. Brookfield, Conn.: Twenty-First Century Books, 2003.

Spangenburg, Ray. *A Look at Saturn*. New York: Franklin Watts, 2002.

FIND OUT MORE AND GET UPDATES

PLANET-WATCHING WEB SITES

StarDate Online: Solar System Guide.
        http://www.stardate.org/resources/ssguide/saturn.html

NightSky Sky Calendar.
        http://www.space.com/spacewatch/sky_calendar.html

SATURN EXPLORATION WEB SITES

Cassini-Huygens Kids.
        http://saturn.jpl.nasa.gov/kids/

The Voyager Missions.
        http://voyager.jpl.nasa.gov/

SOLAR SYSTEM WEB SITES

Solar System Exploration.
        http://solarsystem.nasa.gov/kids/

Windows to the Universe.
        http://www.windows.ucar.edu/tour/link=/saturn/saturn.html

HUYGENS LANDING ON TITAN MOVIE

    http://saturn.jpl.nasa.gov/video/?category=14

Index

A

atmosphere, 34

C

Cassini, 7–19, 28, 30–33, 39
Cassini, Giovanni, 11
clouds, 17
composition, 6

D

Dione, 27, 30, 33

E

Enceladus, 26–27, 30, 33, 42
Encke Gap, 33
Epimetheus, 33

G

Gagarin, Yuri, 33
Galilei, Galileo, 7
gas giants, 6
geysers, 29–31

H

hexagon storm, 18–19
hurricanes, 19
Huygens, 33, 36–39
Huygens, Christiaan, 7, 32, 37
Hyperion, 27

I

Iapetus, 27

J

Janus, 33
Jupiter, 14

L

life, sustaining, 13, 30, 39, 42

M

methane, 38
Mimas, 27, 33
moons
    composition of, 6
    discovery of, 5
    orbits, switching, 33
    overview, 27–28

N

Neptune, 14

P

Pan, 33
Pandora, 33
Phoebe, 27
Porco, Carolyn, 10, 12–13, 16–19, 30–32, 40
Prometheus, 33

R

Rhea, 27, 32, 33
rings, 5–7
    exploration of, 10–16
Rhea, 32

S

space probes, 7–19, 33
"storm alley," 18
storms, 18–19

T

temperatures, 17
Thethys, 27, 33
Titan, 26–27, 32–39, 42–43
Titan Saturn System Mission (TSSM), 42–43

V

Voyager 1 and 2, 14, 18, 26–28, 32, 34

W

weather, 17–19
winds, 17

Z

Zarnecki, John, 33–34, 38, 39